The B
Herb Book

How to Grow, Preserve, and Enjoy Culinary Herbs

Josephine DeFalco

Flint Hills Publishing

Flint Hills Publishing

Topeka, Kansas

www.flinthillspublishing.com

Printed in the U.S.A.

ISBN-13:978-1548114886
ISBN-10:154811488X

Table of Contents

THE ALLURE OF HERBS

Walk into any herb garden after a fresh rain and it doesn't take long for the spicy, pungent fragrance of the herbs to grab your attention. These unique plants can bring to mind memories of family meals and traditional foods. I cannot walk past a basil plant without thinking of my mother's homemade pasta sauce. She would begin her sauce by sautéing onions and garlic in olive oil. While the onions cooked, she walked to the garden box outside her kitchen window and picked her parsley for the meatballs and basil for the sauce. As the day came to a close, our home was filled with delicious smells and no one had to be called to dinner. Everyone was hovering in the kitchen waiting for the food to fill the dining table.

I have a special garden for my herbs on the north side of the house where they are protected from the burning summer sun of the Southwest and the ground retains moisture. That is not to say that herbs are fussy about where they grow. Most require minimum attention to the soils they live in, and in my mild Arizona-winter climate, many herbs are perennials, meaning they survive the winter and add new growth in the spring. At the end of summer or fall when herbs are bushy and strong, I collect selected stems or leaves and process them for storage. If flowers go to seed, those seeds are saved for future plantings. It is a beautiful dance of time—the beginning of life, growth and fruition, harvest, and then restoration.

HERBAL HISTORY

Historians are unsure about the time when human beings started adding herbs to their food. Food was always in limited supply and it is suggested that herbs may have been used to cover up the odor of spoiled food, meat in particular. Scientific discoveries in the 1980s revealed that Ice Age hunters stored surplus meats in the water under frozen lakes and peat bogs. Expecting there would be leftovers from a butchered mastodon, that meat could keep them alive during the harsh winter months— so the need for food preservation was a matter of life and death.

When scientists reenacted the process of

storing raw meat in icy lake water, it was discovered that the meat remained edible, despite the disgusting outside layer of water-soaked flesh. Once that outer layer was removed, it was ready for dinner. I'm guessing that's when an innovative cook chose to add greens and plants from their surrounding habitat to their cooking to enhance the flavor of stored meat. And there you have the birth of culinary herbs.

Through observation, trial, and error, mankind also learned to use herbs for healing. Chew one herb and it could help your upset stomach—or you could die. Rub a leaf on your wound and it could heal faster or develop an irritating rash. Knowledge was passed down generation to generation until writing became common. Then medical books, and yes, cookbooks, recorded how to blend ingredients consistently to produce the same outcome.

GROWING HERBS

Anyone who has ever bought herbs in a grocery store quickly realizes that fresh herbs are expensive. Often, they are not as fresh as we would like and the selection may be limited. How much better would it be to walk out the door and pick your own herbs, wash them, and immediately utilize them in your cooking? It is not hard to collect enough herb plants to make your own fragrant garden and always have a selection of herbs available just outside your door.

Where you decide to plant your herbs will depend on how your property is placed in relation to the sun and your prevailing climate. In the hot, southwest desert that is my home, positioning my herb garden on the north side of the house made the difference between success and failure; for the most part, the plants grow in indirect light. If you live in a cooler, wet climate, your herbs may thrive in full sun. Your smartest move is to talk to an expert at a local nursery as they are happy to support new gardeners. In addition, there are many local gardening groups to be found on the internet. These enthusiastic gardeners provide a wealth of information that they are always willing to share.

If space it tight, it is possible that your herb garden will be arranged in containers, hanging baskets, or a plant tower sitting on your back porch. If you do use a container, remember that heat and cold will be conducted through that container to your plants and may need to be considered when the weather changes. I knew a sweet, little Italian grandma in New Jersey that used to haul her lemon tree out of her basement every spring and pull it back in when fall rolled around. It was a good thing that tree was on wheels and had a special place next to a sunny window.

My experience over the years is that it may take several tries to find a place where your favorite herb will succeed. For example, my thyme did not do well in the sun even during the cooler mornings hours and needed to be moved to a shady spot. To find a home for my sage, I bought two plants and placed them in different environments. They both did well, but I have to say the sage that gets three to four hours of morning sun has grown twice as fast. At my mountain home which is located at a higher elevation, the sage has done very well under the south porch where it gets a little sun but is protected from heavy winter snow.

Herbs are not particular about the soil they grow in and in warm climates, herbs grow year-round. Adding a little mulch and fertilizer to established plants will get new growth off to a good start. I'm all about using natural sources, so a mixture of 50% mulch and 50% manure is a safe choice when mixed in with surrounding soil. Avoid using any fertilizer on new, tender plants.

Unless you are experienced with using fresh

manure—don't! When manure is "hot" or high in nitrogen, it can destroy a garden. Unless you know it has had time to cure and knock down some of that nitrogen, your best bet is to get *composted,* bagged mulch or manure from the nursery. It is important that it is labeled as composted or you could end up with more weeds than herbs. Let me share a recent story about manure.

We were putting in a large field of winter wheat that we normally grow and grind for our baking. Our chickens can't keep up with the demand so I bought the cheapest manure I could find—about 12 bags, and spread it on the field. We planted the field and pretty soon we started seeing greenery come up. We were very excited but the only problem was that it wasn't our wheat. It was a hideous weed, one we had never seen before, and it loved our wheat field! We couldn't keep up with the weeding and before long I couldn't see the wheat for the weeds. This had never occurred before in our raised garden beds. I was furious and called the manure company in west Phoenix. Before the end of the conversation I was well schooled in manure.

The bottom line is most cow manure is dropped from the farmer, bagged, and shipped off to the nursery within three days!

"Three days!" I bellowed. "I might as well have the whole herd roaming in my field to deliver it directly."

The woman on the other end of the phone was actually very understanding. "A lot of people don't know that there is such a fast turn-around," she explained. "Unless it says specifically on that manure bag that it was composted, you run a very high risk of bringing weed seeds and who knows what else, home to plant in your yard. Our manure comes in from all over the place." She went into great detail about composting and how important it was to take the time to buy the good stuff or cook your own with added food and yard waste, heat, and time. It was a good review for me and with the large field I had become compliant and somewhat lazy with my soil conditioning. Composting allows the manure and organic material to heat up and kill most of the seeds that animals consume. Otherwise, undigested seeds come out the other end, are bagged and delivered right to your yard. Our little composting bin was not going to be enough for these larger fields, so yes, next on the agenda is constructing a large, three-section composting area.

By this time there was no way to control the "devil weed" growing in our field. We do not use herbicides and sadly, we had to hang tough and plow under the entire field before it all went to seed and made more weeds. Our next step was to cover the field in heavy black plastic, deny it water, and hope the heat would help destroy any remaining seeds. That seemed to work rather well and when it was time to turn the soil, most of the weeds had been destroyed and we were back to fighting our old friends: Bermuda grass and nutgrass.

So, thank your neighbor for his generous offer of fresh, premium cow manure, but wait until you know how to compost all that good stuff before accepting his gift.

I never add fertilizer of any kind when planting

new herbs. All they need is a little mulch and if your soil is healthy and rich with organic material, you won't need to add anything except a little tender loving care. Once they are established, you can consider adding a little fertilizer once or twice a year.

Enhance your spring herb bed and established plants by lightly digging the soil surrounding the plants. Avoid disturbing the roots. Add a composted mulch/manure mixture to the soil and continue to turn the soil until soil, mulch, and fertilizer are blended. Finish with a deep watering to settle any air pockets and push nutrients toward the roots.

If you live in a cold climate where the plants do not survive winter, why not start your annual plants indoors and have something delicious to look forward to? Plant nurseries and catalogs have seed starting containers and seedling soil specifically made for starting tiny, delicate seeds. An ambitious gardener can start designing her herb garden and be ready to start planting on that first warm, spring day.

PRESERVING HERBS

Most of the herbs presented in this book can be preserved in the same way. Some do not do well when frozen and can darken and lose their flavor. Others dry quickly and some grow year-round so preservation is not needed. They continue to reseed on their own, returning year after year. All you have to do is acknowledge their presence, add a few nutrients, give them some space, and they are on their way for another bountiful season.

Under each specific herb, there is a discussion about processing. Feel free to try different methods of preservation. I have made recommendations based on years of growing experience but that is not to say you won't find a better way. When using fresh herbs in a recipe that calls for a dried herb, use three times as much herb to account for the dehydration. The exception to this is rosemary which does not lose a significant volume after drying.

My favorite new piece of equipment is a multiple-tiered drying rack; The Food Pantrie, that I hang from the eaves outside my shady kitchen window. When summer temperatures reach 115 degrees, that hot wind is perfect for drying herbs and vegetables and the screening keeps the bugs away. I also have a traditional electric food dryer, but sometimes it can take several days for drying to be completed and food can mold if you do not allow ample spacing. That doesn't happen when Mother Nature is doing the work with free, solar energy.

In time, you will find what works best for you and your family. The next section, *Tools to Process Herbs*, provides information on some of the gadgets I use to make my herb preservation and processing a little easier.

TOOLS TO GROW, PROCESS, AND PRESERVE HERBS

These items can be found online or at local gourmet kitchen stores. Sometimes I can find interesting tools at reasonable prices at restaurant supply stores. Some of these gadgets are just plain fun to use and can save a lot of time.

Herb Scissors with 5 blades- Herb scissors make chopping herbs easy in half the time. Any large, leafy herb can be trimmed in preparation for drying and because it is a simple hand tool, you can maneuver around stems.

Salad spinner- If you have a salad spinner to remove moisture from you washed greens, it can also be used to remove water from your herbs before drying or hanging. There are even small spinners just for herbs. Kids love to help with this task, so put them to work!

Chef'n Zipstrip Herb Zipper- This is used to strip small leaves off tough, woody stems like rosemary, sage, oregano, and lavender. Push the stem through a little hole and pull back. The herb leaves collect in the attached bowl, ready for your next recipe.

Herb Mill with Herb Stripper- Herbs are pushed through a mill with a twist of the hand and multiple blades cut the leaves to size. A stripper is built into the mill to remove leaves from stems.

Mortar and Pestle- Don't overlook this common tool. It is great for muddling herbs (like mint for Mojitos) or bringing out the essential oils in any herb before preparing a recipe.

Coffee and Spice Grinder- There are many versions of these electric grinders on the market. They do a great job, are relatively easy to clean, and have built-in safety features to make the job fast and easy.

Sachet or stock bags for bouquet garni- Keep a few of these small muslin bags on hand to hold fresh herbs that can be dropped into stock, soups, or stews. They add all the flavor but save you from picking the stems and leaves out of your creations.

Cutting Globes- I discovered these at Baker Creek Seed Company's annual Spring Festival in Mansfield, Missouri. Multi-sized plastic containers attach a ball of dirt and moisture directly to your herb branch. In six weeks after roots have developed, snip off the stem and you have propagated a new herb plant for your garden or one to share with someone else. So much fun! There are endless ways to use this tool.

STARTING YOUR GARDEN

This book covers some of the easiest herbs to grow. Once you have mastered these herbs, expand your garden a little each year. In the future, you might be interested in growing borage, horseradish, or lavender. Wander around your local plant nursery and see what intrigues you. Mother Nature's offerings are endless.

Basil

Description: Basil is often one of the fresh herbs you will find in the grocery store, probably because of its popularity and versatility. It is also sold as a dry herb. Any leftover fresh herbs that are not used immediately may be dried and used later.

Growing and Maintenance of Basil

There are so many different kinds of basil: lemon, chocolate, lime, cinnamon, Thai, sweet, holy—the list goes on and on. If you want to start with the basic variety, choose sweet basil.

This plant practically grows itself. In fact, it is so well adapted to our little farm that it reseeds itself every year. I thin the planting box down to two or three strong plants, sometimes supporting them with a wire tomato cage. Water regularly and if necessary, add mulch and fertilizer once the plants are about a foot tall. These plants rarely face pests, although whiteflies have sometimes been a problem. If you see a sticky substance on your leaves, any kind of wilting, or small flies when you touch the plant, you have an infestation. I usually hose the basil and the offenders down once a day and if things do not improve, then I bring out the Neem oil which suffocates the insects and larvae. To be effective, the oil must come in contact with the insects that are usually hiding on the underside of the leaves. Neem oil is not a chemical and is considered to be an organic product.

Some gardeners like to use sticky, yellow cards or tape that attract the insects. That is where they die. However, I have had the unfortunate experience of having to remove a small, live sparrow from a yellow card which was completely nerve-wracking for both me and the bird. I am happy to say that the bird flew away after I spent thirty minutes cutting away at feathers with a hand-held razor blade. I have also seen the same fate for lizards and geckos, always too late for me to make a rescue. For this reason, these products are not a part of my garden pest control.

Harvesting Basil

Harvesting basil is a happy time for me. Late in the summer the basil begins to put out small white flowers. This makes the bees very busy and soon seeds are forming in little pockets. I save a few of the flowering stems to produce seeds for next year. When the flowers are gone and the flowering tips of the basil bush are brown, I pinch off a few of these browned flowers and roll them in the palm of my hand. Little black seeds will remain behind and these can be saved for next year's planting. Be sure they are completely dry before harvesting and storing.

As for the basil leaves themselves, there are so many different ways to preserve this herb. I start by cutting large branches and spraying them with cool water to remove any soil, dust, and wayward insects. Home gardeners probably clean their herbs much better than anything grown commercially, so take comfort in that thought.

Preservation of Basil

The simplest way to dry basil is to gather up the large branches into a small bundle, tie with twine or string, shake off the excess moisture, and hang in a dry, dark place. By dark, I mean not in direct sunlight. We use our garage where there is very little dust (we get dust storms all summer long). It is dry and safe from insects. At this time, I pick off any unsightly leaves that do not meet my expectations. When the leaves are crispy it's time to collect the dried basil. I lay out newspaper or paper towels on a clean, flat surface, preferably outside. One at a time the bundles are rolled, compressed, and "massaged" to get the leaves off the branches. Remove any stems and pack in airtight jars. If necessary, I finish crushing them later when they are being used in cooking.

Another choice is to pick the leaves off the branches, sorting out the good leaves. I put the leaves in a large bowl filled with cool water. The leaves go through several washes until the water is nearly clean. Drain the water from the basil. Use a salad spinner to cast off as much water as possible. Scatter the leaves in a thin layer on a baking sheet or clean counter. Then ignore them until they are dry. This could take several days or even a couple of weeks if you live in a humid environment.

Leaves may be frozen from a fresh state and used later in cooked products. After rinsing leaves, mince and freeze in ice cube trays. You can easily remove the number of cubes needed for a recipe.

Plastic bags will work too. I fill the sandwich bags with a moderate portion of minced herbs, push out all the air, and flatten the bag to one-fourth of an inch before freezing. When you need herbs it's easy to break off a chunk and refreeze the rest.

Basil Uses

⚜ Rub a fresh basil leaf on an insect bite to reduce inflammation.

⚜ Add basil to sauces, dips, and fresh salads. Basil is great with bruschetta, a thin slice of mozzarella cheese, and balsamic vinegar. Top pizza dough with fresh tomato slices, fresh basil, mozzarella cheese, and olive oil for a vegetarian margherita pizza.

⚜ Pierce roasting meats with a sharp knife and push basil leaves into the opening. Roast as directed. Delicious!

Basil Recipes

Basil Pesto

The basil in our gardens grows wild and every year we end up with fresh basil growing everywhere. This basil pesto freezes well and can be added to any pasta sauce to enhance the flavor. We use small, 8-ounce freezer containers and take out what we need during the winter. Pesto can also be frozen in ice cube trays and stored in freezer bags. Note: If you plan to freeze your pesto, eliminate the cheese and add it at the time you are serving. Adding a tablespoon of lemon juice will prevent the pesto from darkening during storage.

2 cups **fresh basil leaves**, packed

⅓ cup pine nuts or walnuts

3 garlic cloves, coarsely chopped

½ cup virgin olive oil

½ cup Parmesan cheese

Salt and pepper to taste

Combine basil, nuts, and garlic in food processor and pulse to chop ingredients into smaller pieces. Turn on processor and drizzle oil into funnel until blended. Remove from processor and stir in cheese. Toss with hot pasta and serve. This pesto may also be used as a spread when preparing bruschetta. Makes 1 cup.

❦❦❦

Marinated Vegetable Salad

This colorful salad utilizes all the fresh summer vegetables at the market. If you do not want to make your own salad dressing, any French dressing will make a good substitute. Did you know that mustard acts as an emulsifier in any salad dressing and will help to blend the oil and vinegar for a homogenous dressing?

An easy way to slice fresh basil is to roll several leaves together and slice in the opposite direction. Separate strips and you will have julienne basil to add to your recipe.

First, prepare the salad dressing by combining the following ingredients:

1 cup extra virgin olive oil

1 tablespoon prepared mustard

¼ cup ketchup

1 tablespoon honey

Salt and pepper to taste

1 green pepper, diced

1 yellow pepper, diced

½ red onion, sliced thin

2-3 stalks celery, cut into ½ inch pieces

2 medium zucchinis

1 cup broccoli florets

1 cup sliced carrots

1 cup cauliflower florets

1 cup grape or cherry tomatoes, halved

5-6 **fresh basil leaves** (or more) sliced into thin strips

1½ tablespoons **fresh oregano** or 1½ teaspoons dried oregano

Salt and pepper to taste

Prepare peppers, onion, and celery as listed and place in large bowl. Bring salted water to boil in a

3-quart pot. Prepare a separate bowl with ice and water to cool blanched vegetables.

When the water comes to a boil add zucchini, broccoli, carrots, and cauliflower. Continue to boil for 1-2 minutes. Immediately remove vegetables from boiling water and place in ice water. When cool, drain well and add to peppers, onion, and celery. Add tomatoes, oregano and basil. Drizzle dressing over salad and mix gently until vegetables are evenly coated. Refrigerate 2 hours before serving. Makes 10-12 servings.

🌾🌾🌾

Nana's Sugo

When I was a young girl I remember walking home from school during the winter months and seeing the windows in the kitchen steamed with humidity. That told me that Mom was making pasta for dinner and a pot of boiling water was on the stove. Right next to it was a fragrant kettle of pasta sauce. When I finally walked in the door I was surrounded with the heavenly smells of onion, garlic, oregano, and basil. This is her recipe as it has been made for the last 50 years.

3 tablespoons virgin olive oil

4 cloves garlic, sliced or minced

¾ cup onion, chopped

12 ounces tomato paste

28 ounces tomato puree

3 cups water

1 teaspoon **dried basil**

¼ cup red wine

2½ teaspoons salt

¾ teaspoon sugar

Black pepper to taste

Optional: a piece of beef, pork, or meatballs may be simmered with this sauce for extra flavor and later served with the pasta.

In a large, heavy-bottom pot, heat oil and sauté onion and garlic until translucent, about 5 minutes. Add remaining ingredients, blend, and simmer uncovered on low for 1½ hours or until sauce reaches desired thickness. Makes about 5 cups.

.

BAY LAUREL

Description: Bay Laurel is usually found in stores as a dark green leaf. It can also be ground into a powder. Bay grows on a bush which easily grows into a tree. That means as soon as you can spare a few leaves off your new bay laurel plant, you can start using your herb.

Growing and Maintenance of Bay Laurel

There is a lot of discussion over which planting zones are compatible with bay trees. Some say don't plant them in zones less than seven, others report they do best in zones five through nine. My suggestion is to evaluate your own microclimate.

A microclimate is an area that produces slightly different weather conditions, despite local, general predictions. For example, in my area we are about seven degrees cooler than the rest of the urban area and our humidity is higher. Both the seeds that we save from our heirloom plants and our perennial plants have adapted to our microclimate. At the end of the season when I harvest the best seeds, those seeds are genetically programmed to be the best producers in my microclimate.

If it gets below freezing on a regular basis, bay laurel needs to be potted in a container. This will allow you to move your plant indoors when the weather changes. Put your container on a wheel platform and you can move it anywhere! To keep your bay from growing into a thirty-foot tree, trim and shape it each spring. Make it a part of your outdoor décor by planting it in a bright container and shaping it like a topiary or oversized bonsai tree.

If you live in a warm climate where it seldom freezes, plant your bay bush where it will get at least four hours of shade or filtered light. Allow room for vertical growth. My desert climate can reach temperatures of over 115 degrees during the summer, so it is important to protect my bay from sunburn. Our bay laurel is planted east of a row of tall, Japanese privet bushes so the west sun cannot damage the leaves. Water your bay regularly but do not allow it to sit in soggy soil.

Harvesting Bay Laurel

Harvesting is as easy as picking leaves off the tree. Fragrant, tender leaves are more potent.

Bay Laurel Preservation

After harvesting the leaves, wash in cool water to remove dust and debris. I select the best leaves and lay them out on a baking sheet or clean surface to dry until brittle. Whole leaves can be stored in airtight containers.

To make bay laurel into a powder you will need some patience. Putting them in a food processor or blender just pushes the stiff leaf pieces around the container. I break or chop my leaves into smaller pieces and use a small coffee grinder or my grain mill to pulverize my herb.

Bay Laurel Uses

❧ Do not eat whole bay leaves. Chewing a bay leaf will result in small, sharp pieces that can damage your digestive system. Remove whole leaves before serving or use as a powder.

❧ Bay has been used for time and eternity to ease digestive problems. My grandmother boiled bay leaf in a small amount of water, added a little sugar, cooled the water, put it in a baby bottle and gave it to a colicky baby to ease gas bubbles. Today we do not recommend putting sugar in a baby's bottle, but tell that to a mother that has not slept all night!

❧ Bay can act as an insect repellant. Store a few whole leaves on pantry shelves or with dry goods to drive away moths and weevils.

Bay Laurel Recipes

Beef Burgundy

This dish can be prepared in a crock pot and waiting for you at the end of a long day. Serve with fresh French bread and a green salad with blue cheese dressing. Make dinner even easier by using a crock liner for fast clean-up.

1 pound sliced mushrooms

2 cloves garlic, minced

1 tablespoon butter

3 slices bacon, cooked crisp and crumbled (save bacon fat)

¾ cup flour

½ teaspoon seasoned salt

1½ pounds stew meat

10 ounces beef broth

1 teaspoon **dried thyme**

1 tablespoon tomato paste

2-3 **bay leaves**

10 small peeled onions or 2 medium onions, quartered

1 cup carrots, peeled and sliced diagonally, about 2 carrots

½ cup burgundy wine with prepared mushrooms

In a medium to large skillet, sauté mushrooms and garlic in butter. Remove and set aside. In the same pan, cook bacon until crispy. Remove, cool and crumble, set aside.

In a small bowl or plastic bag, combine flour and seasoned salt. Add beef and shake to coat. Brown meat in bacon fat. Place meat in crockpot and set on low heat. Combine broth, thyme, and tomato paste and pour over beef. Add bay leaves, onions, carrots, and bacon. Cook for 8-9 hours. During the last hour of cooking add mushroom, garlic, and wine. Remove bay leaves before serving. Makes 4-5 servings.

Shrimp Creole

Shrimp cooks quickly! Once the shrimp has been added to a recipe it takes 5-7 minutes (depending on the size of the shrimp) to finish cooking. When shrimp turns pink and begins to curve into a "C," it is nearly done. To insure the shrimp cooks evenly if it is frozen, defrost completely before adding it to a recipe.

3 tablespoons coconut oil

1 cup celery, chopped, about 3 stalks

1 cup onions, sliced, about 1 small onion

1 cup green pepper, cut into strips, about 2 peppers

32 ounces diced tomatoes

8 ounces tomato sauce

2 **bay leaves**

1 tablespoon salt

1 tablespoon sugar

1 tablespoon chili powder

¼ teaspoon hot sauce or to taste

1 pound cleaned shrimp

2 tablespoons flour

¼ cup water

In a large skillet, heat oil and sauté onions, peppers, and celery until translucent, about 10 minutes. Add tomatoes and tomato sauce, bay leaves, salt, sugar, chili powder, and hot sauce. Cover, reduce heat and simmer for 20 minutes. Add shrimp and continue cooking on low heat for 5-10 minutes or until shrimp turns pink.

Make a slurry of flour and water and add to ingredients, stirring constantly to blend into sauce. When mixture thickens and flour is cooked, remove bay leaves. Serve over rice. Makes 4 servings.

❧❧❧

Vegetable Barley Soup

A hearty winter soup that has been a family favorite for years.

1 pound mushrooms, sliced

6 tablespoons butter, divided

½ cup barley

1 cup onion, chopped, about 1 medium onion

2 garlic cloves, minced

1 cup carrots, about 3 carrots, peeled and chopped

1 cup celery, about 3 stalks celery chopped

3 tablespoons flour

8 cups beef broth

15-16 ounces diced canned tomatoes

1 cup tomato puree

2 tablespoons tomato paste

1 teaspoon salt

½ teaspoon black pepper

3 **bay leaves**

3 tablespoons **fresh parsley**, chopped

3 tablespoons sherry

1 cup sour cream

In a large saucepan, melt butter and sauté mushrooms in 3 tablespoons of butter until mushroom liquid is reduced. Remove and set aside. In the same pan, parboil barley for 30 minutes, drain and set aside.

Add remaining butter to saucepan and sauté onion, garlic, carrots, and celery for 5 minutes. Stir in flour until mixture thickens and liquid is absorbed.

Add beef broth, canned tomatoes, tomato puree, tomato paste, salt, pepper, bay leaves, and parboiled barley. Reduce heat, cover, and simmer for 30 minutes or until barley is tender.

Add parsley and sherry and simmer another 3-5 minutes to blend flavors. Remove bay leaves before serving. To serve, ladle into bowls and top with a dollop of sour cream. Makes 8-10 servings.

CILANTRO

Description: Cilantro is a leafy herb, similar in appearance to parsley, and a must to make authentic Mexican food. Its unique flavor and aroma is always served as a fresh green. I have tried drying cilantro to use during our hot summer months when it does not grow in the desert and can tell you not to waste your time. With cilantro, it's fresh or nothing!

Growing and Maintenance of Cilantro

Cilantro is very sensitive to seasonal temperatures. But give it what it wants and it performs beautifully. It likes the sun, but does not do well in temperatures that are too hot. It will "bolt" quickly, meaning it will start to produce flowers and go to seed. When I plant it, I apply a generous portion of seeds, making sure they are sprinkled with water every day until the sprouts emerge. Thereafter, they get watered with the rest of the garden. I routinely protect all new sprouts with small wire cages as the birds like my tender greens as much as I do!

Making wire cages is not difficult but you do need to wear gloves to protect your hands and long sleeves to protect your arms. Purchase half-inch chicken wire at any feed store. You will not find this size at a regular hardware or big-box store. Cut the wire into the length that is needed, adding twelve to sixteen inches for the end enclosures. Arch the wire like you are making a small hut over your seedlings. Overlap the ends so the birds cannot find their way under the cover and arrange over your seeded row. As soon as the seedlings are touching the top of the arch, I take it away knowing it is safe from herbivores. I use these wire cages with any seedlings when I have concerns about it being a delectable meal for animals.

In addition, this same half-inch chicken wire is great to line the bottom of my raised beds as they are being constructed. This discourages moles and gophers. In truth, they can chew threw the wire, but most give up before they resort to that much work. One time I was constructing a new box and several days passed after I had lined the bed with chicken wire. I returned to find a three-inch hole under the wire with a protruding bulge exactly the same size as a gopher's head. I am sure somewhere in my back yard there was a rodent with a terrible headache and an empty stomach!

Harvesting Cilantro

Cilantro will continue to produce as long as the environment cooperates. When harvesting, I take a sharp knife and cut out a section of greens close to the soil thereby allowing room for new growth. I move along the row of herbs, selecting a new section and taking only what I need each time I harvest. Once the plants begin to flower, the leaves get small and tasteless and cilantro season is over.

Cilantro Preservation

Wash the cilantro in cool water prior to chopping. Only the leaves on the cilantro are used for cooking; the stems are discarded or added to the compost pile. We usually use whole cilantro leaves or keep the pieces fairly large. Use your own judgement when preparing your recipes. Fresh cilantro does not freeze well and tastes a little bit like grass after it is defrosted—not very appealing. When cilantro is dried, it loses all its flavor and becomes very bland. Perhaps this is why gardeners get so upset when cilantro season is over as it is not an herb that can be preserved.

Cilantro Uses

⚜ When making a cheese crisp, top a flour tortilla with whole cilantro leaves and cover with cheddar cheese before broiling.

⚜ If a cilantro plant flowers and goes to seed, the resulting seeds are known as coriander. Not only can they produce next year's cilantro, but coriander is a spice that can be ground and used in cooking with a completely different flavor.

⚜ Papalo, also known as skunkweed, is sometimes used as a summer cilantro as it tolerates heat without a problem. Try it as an alternative to cilantro if you live in a hot, arid area and crave cilantro during the summer.

Cilantro Recipes

Erin's Classic Tomato Salsa

For as long as I can remember, Erin's salsa has been a staple at our family gatherings. We have had it for a July 4th costume party, Christmas, and even bachelorette parties. Make extra as it will not last long. And don't forget the tortilla chips!

4 cups Roma tomatoes, diced, or 32 ounces canned diced or crushed tomatoes with garlic and oregano, drained

8 ounces fresh or canned peppers, drained: green chili, jalapeño, serrano, etc.

¼ cup sliced scallions, about 2-3 scallions (green onions)

1 clove garlic, minced

Juice from one large lime

1 cup **cilantro,** packed and chopped fine

Recommended: 1-2 tablespoons liquid from pickled pepperoncini peppers

Salt and pepper to taste

Mix all ingredients. Taste improves if it is prepared the day before.

❧❧❧

Green Salsa

16 ounces Salsa Verde, Herdez brand preferred

1 cup **cilantro**, packed

2 garlic cloves, minced

Juice from 1 lemon

½ jalapeño, seeded or unseeded (seeds will make your salsa hotter)

Salt and pepper

Combine all ingredients in a blender or food processor and process to desired consistency.

≋≋≋

Orange Salsa

5 plum tomatoes, diced

¼ cup scallions, about 2 onions, sliced thin

Juice from 1 lime

1 garlic clove, minced

Jalapeño or serrano pepper, diced

1 cup **cilantro**, packed and chopped fine

22 ounces mandarin oranges in light syrup, drained, coarsely chopped

1-2 teaspoons salt, divided

Optional: ¼ to ½ cup Triple Sec

Place tomatoes in a colander or sieve, sprinkle with 1 teaspoon salt and mix. Allow tomatoes to drain for about 10 minutes and discard excess liquid. Combine tomatoes, scallions, lime, garlic, pepper, cilantro, and the oranges. Salt and pepper to taste. Add Triple Sec and marinate overnight.

🌾🌾🌾

Fish Tacos

(Of course, these fish tacos go great with Erin's Salsa.)

2-pound mild, white fish such as cod or orange roughy, cut into one-inch strips down the length of the fillet

oil for frying (my preference for deep frying is sunflower oil)

Batter:

1¼ cup beer

1egg

1 cup flour

1 teaspoon sugar

¼ teaspoon salt

Old Bay seasoning

About 8 flour or corn tortillas

Toppings:

Lime wedges

Grated cheddar cheese

Diced tomatoes

Shredded cabbage

Cilantro

Sauce:

Equal parts of your favorite salsa and mayonnaise

In a small bowl, beat the egg with beer. Add flour, sugar, and salt. Using a fork, beat mixture to make a smooth batter.

Prepare a large frying pan with oil and heat. Test oil heat by dropping a small amount of batter in the pan. A quick sizzle means it is ready. Lower fish strips into hot cooking oil, one at a time, allowing excess batter to drain from the fish before frying.

Fry fish strips in hot oil until crispy and brown and fish flakes easily. Cook no more than two or three minutes on each side. Use a medium high temperature and do not allow oil to smoke. Drain on paper towels and sprinkle with Old Bay.

Place fillet in tortilla, drizzle with lime juice and top with suggested ingredients. Add additional toppings and sauce as desired. Finish meal with a side of seasoned pinto beans.

※※※

Tomato Cilantro Appetizer

1½ sheets phyllo dough

¼ cup mayonnaise

1 tablespoon Sriracha sauce

8 ounces Monterey Jack cheese, shredded

8 plum tomatoes, sliced thin

¾ cup **cilantro**, chopped

1½ tablespoons dried **oregano**

½ teaspoon salt

¼ teaspoon red pepper flakes

1½ tablespoons **sage**

½ cup olive oil

3 cloves garlic, minced

Roll out phyllo dough onto a 12 x 18-inch, greased baking pan. Combine Sriracha sauce with mayonnaise and brush dough with sauce. Sprinkle with cheese followed by cilantro and sliced tomatoes.

In a small bowl, combine oregano, salt, pepper flakes, sage, olive oil, and garlic. Drizzle over dough. Bake at 375 degrees for 10-15 minutes or until pastry is medium brown. Cut into squares. Serve warm or at room temperature. Makes 48 appetizers.

DILL

Description: Dill is a feathery, fragrant herb and both the green lacey leaves and seeds can be used in food preparation. In the desert, it is a cool weather crop and grown in winter and spring. In other parts of the United States it is grown during the summer months.

Growing and Maintenance of Dill

My only complaint about growing dill in the desert is that it grows in the winter when I need it in the summer! While the summer cucumbers are bountiful and screaming to be preserved for dill pickles, it is too hot to grow dill. I have had marginal success growing it in the shade of summer plants—like tomatoes—but eventually the heat wins at that game. If you are lucky enough to live in a climate where cucumbers and dill grows at the same time, make sure delicious dills are in your future.

Plant dill seeds in a shallow trench, rich with composted soil. Sprinkle daily until the seeds sprout and then water in conjunction with your regular schedule. I rarely thin my plants but instead, let them take their own path. Long stems may try to fall over and if this is the case, they can be staked with poles to help them remain upright.

Dill plants will flower into a six to eight-inch circular seed head. If your objective is to collect the seeds, I recommend Mammoth Dill which will produce very large seeds. But watch the birds as they love the seeds and can clean a seed head in just a couple of days. You can take grandma's old nylon stockings or any porous netting to make a hat over the seed head and discourage hungry birds. This also works quite well with sunflowers if you are planning to collect the seeds for yourself.

Harvesting Dill

The feathery leaves from the dill plant can be harvested and used fresh once the plant has grown to a substantial size. Use scissors to trim the leaves, harvesting only what you can use immediately.

If harvesting for preservation, use gardening shears or a sharp knife to cut the entire stalk. Gently rinse the delicate herb, shake to remove excess water. Tie and hang for drying.

To collect dill seeds, wait until the seed head has turned brown. To insure you collect all your seeds, bend your seed head into a plastic grocery bag or paper sack before cutting it from the stalk.

Dill Preservation

It should not take long for this herb to dry. It can be processed the same way as basil, rolling in newspaper or paper towels to loosen the herb from the stalk. Store dried dill in jars or air-tight containers.

If the seeds have not fallen off the seed head, I pinch them off the stalk. Little pieces of stems may remain behind. To remove these, I rub the seeds between my palms. A large, old strainer is a great tool to shake off any unwanted plant stems, leaving behind your delicious seeds.

Dill Uses

❧ Planting dill with broccoli and cauliflower will draw aphids away from your vegetables.

❧ Use fresh, chopped dill in green salads, tuna salad or chicken salad for a unique, fresh flavor.

❧ Sauté fresh chopped dill in butter and add to boiled new potatoes.

❧ While making scrambled eggs, add fresh dill; use dill as a garnish for deviled eggs.

Dill Recipes

Fish Amandine

Traditionally this recipe is prepared with trout, but any fish—halibut, seabass, or my favorite, barramundi, is equally delicious. When purchasing your fish, buy 6-8 ounces per serving.

¼ cup butter

½ cup slivered almonds

1 pound salmon fillets

1 teaspoon **fresh parsley**, chopped

¼ teaspoon salt

¼ teaspoon lemon pepper

1½ teaspoons **fresh dill**

In a large frying pan, melt butter and sauté almonds until they are golden brown. Remove from pan and set aside.

Place fish in pan and turn to coat both sides in butter. If fish has a skin, place skin side down. Sprinkle with parsley, salt, lemon pepper, and dill. Cook for 2-3 minutes on each side or until fillet flakes easily with a fork. Top with toasted almonds. Serve with lemon wedges. Makes 2 servings.

Lamb with Dill Sauce

Lamb chops and rice make a great dinner combination. Try brown rice for added nutrition and a nutty flavor.

3 tablespoons coconut or cooking oil

½ cup onion, diced

4 lamb chops, ½ inch thick

2 tablespoons water

1 tablespoon vinegar

½ teaspoon salt

¼ teaspoon black pepper

2-3 **bay leaves**

Dill sauce:

2 tablespoons butter

2 tablespoons flour

¼ teaspoon salt

½ cup prepared vegetable broth

2 tablespoons chopped **fresh dill**

½ cup white wine

In a large skillet, heat oil and sauté onions until lightly browned and translucent. Set aside. In the same skillet, brown chops. Add water, vinegar, salt, pepper, and bay leaves. Add onions, cover, and cook on low heat until chops are tender, about 25 minutes. Discard bay leaves.

While chops cook, prepare the sauce. Melt butter and add flour to make a roux. Cook until roux is lightly brown, then add salt, broth, dill, and continue cooking until sauce thickens. Remove from heat and add wine.

To serve, plate rice, arrange lamb in center of rice and top with dill sauce.

🌿🌿🌿

Brunch Biscuits

To prepare this recipe you will need large muffin tins.

10 canned biscuits

8 ounce fully cooked sausages

2 ounces grated cheddar cheese, about ½ cup

3 eggs, beaten

2 tablespoons milk

2 tablespoons **fresh dill**

On a lightly floured board, roll biscuits to a 4 to 5-inch diameter. Lay over greased muffin cup. Fill with one sausage cut in half and two tablespoons grated cheese.

Beat eggs with milk and using a ladle, fill muffin tins equally, saving about 1 tablespoon of egg. Sprinkle with dill. Pinch together top of biscuit and twist to close. Brush with remaining beaten egg. Bake at 400 degrees for 10-12 minutes. Makes 10 biscuits.

FENNEL

Description: Fennel and dill are so similar in appearance that I often have to pinch off a small piece and smell it to determine which is which. Fennel leaves, bulbs, and seed can be used in food preparation. Fennel develops a large, white bulb near the soil line and this can be harvested and sliced like celery, eaten raw, or cooked with foods for a delicate, licorice flavor. Fennel seeds are often used in Italian cooking.

Growing and Maintenance of Fennel

Once fennel is established in your garden, it will reseed and return year after year. To start fennel seeds, make a shallow trench and scatter seeds to a depth of four times the size of the seed. Lightly sprinkle with water until seedlings emerge. Keeping in mind that fennel bulbs will grow to a width of three to four inches, thin out the seedlings so only the strongest plants remain at least two inches apart. Even if the seeds are what you are after, it is advised to thin your plants.

Harvesting Fennel

Fennel grows slowly so allow three to four months before you harvest the bulb developing at the base of the plant. Do not allow your fennel bulb to get too large as it gets tough and becomes inedible; harvest when it is less than three inches in diameter. If one or two sneaks by you, go ahead and allow it to flower and it will produce seeds for seasoning and planting. When you are ready to harvest, use a sharp knife to cut close to the base of the plant. Trim any stems extending from the bulb and disc.

Fennel Preservation

Fennel bulbs that are washed and sliced can be stored in the refrigerator for a couple of weeks before they begin to darken and become unappetizing. When there is surplus fennel, I wash, slice, and store in freezer bags to use in cooking. Fennel seeds are produced the same way as dill. Protect the heads from hungry birds and allow seeds to dry on the plant before harvesting.

Fennel Uses

⚜ The delicate leaves on the fennel plant can be trimmed off the stem and used in salads, dips, or as a garnish.

⚜ Young fennel bulbs can be eaten raw and used for dipping to replace potato chips.

⚜ Fennel seeds are a delicious addition to meatballs or sausage recipes.

⚜ Iron and the amino acid histidine, both found in fennel, are helpful in the treatment of anemia.

Fennel Recipes

Chicken with Fennel

3 tablespoons virgin olive oil

1 **fennel bulb** cut into ½ inch slices

1 cup onion, sliced, about 1 medium onion

8 chicken thighs

3 cloves garlic, sliced

1 cup chicken broth

½ cup white wine

1 tablespoon tomato paste

1 teaspoon salt

Black pepper to taste

1 tablespoon flour

2 tablespoons water

In a large frying pan, heat olive oil and sauté fennel and onion until translucent and soft, about 10 minutes. Remove and set aside.

Brown chicken with garlic in pan drippings. In a small bowl, combine broth, wine, tomato paste, salt and pepper, and add to chicken. Return fennel and onion to pan, cover and simmer for 30 minutes or until chicken is no longer pink.

Make a slurry of flour and water and add to chicken. Allow flour to cook and sauce to thicken. To serve, plate chicken and top with vegetables and sauce. Serve with a side dish of polenta or gnocchi. Makes 6-8 servings.

☙☙☙

Italian Sausage

Making sausage at my house was a big deal when I was a kid. Mom and Dad would make pounds of sausage, wrap it in freezer paper, label it with family names, and use it for Christmas presents for all their friends. This is an abbreviated version of their recipe that can be frozen into logs or made into patties. A good sausage will have a fat content of at least a 30 percent. I know it sounds like a lot and the fat content can be reduced for personal taste, but you run the risk of having a dry, mealy product.

Sausage is great prepared as a breakfast meat,

mixed into meatballs, or used in sauces. You will need a meat grinder to prepare this recipe, either a manual version or electric.

18-20 pounds fresh Boston butt pork shoulder; fat and bone content will vary but you should have at least 12 pounds of useable meat after trimming. Save the bones for soup.

6 tablespoons salt

2 tablespoons black pepper

3½ tablespoons whole **fennel seed**

1 cup red wine (and some extra for the sausage maker!)

The night before making the sausage, trim pork of bone and large pieces of fat. Allow some fat for the sausage (30%). Cut into 1-inch pieces. In a large bowl, combine pork, salt, pepper fennel, and wine. Cover and let marinate overnight, stirring on several occasions.

The next day set up the grinder. Usually you have a choice of a medium or fine grind. Grind a small amount of meat to cook a test patty. This was the best part of the event as it inevitably started a heated debate about seasonings, fat content, etc. If it wasn't too early in the day, it also involved more wine. Adjust seasonings at this time.

After grinding, divide meat into desired portions, wrap in freezer paper, label and date. This meat should keep for at least six months in the freezer.

≝ ≝ ≝

Roasted Fennel Bulbs

This is a wonderful side dish for pork.

2 **fennel bulbs**, sliced into wedges or quartered

1 tablespoon virgin olive oil

Salt and pepper to taste

Juice from one lemon

Oil a 13x9-inch baking pan. Place fennel in a small bowl and drizzle with olive oil. Toss to coat pieces evenly with oil. Salt and pepper fennel and drizzle with lemon juice. Arrange on baking pan and bake at 375 degrees for 30 minutes. Turn wedges every 10-15 minutes to brown on all sides. Makes 4 servings.

☙☙☙

Sausage with Cabbage and Fennel

4 tablespoons butter

1 small cabbage, coarsely chopped

1 small onion, chopped

1 **fennel bulb**, sliced

1 pound smoked sausage or kielbasa, sliced diagonally into 1-inch pieces

15 ounces canned tomatoes

Salt and pepper to taste

In a large skillet melt butter. Add cabbage, onion, and fennel and sauté until vegetables are tender, about 10 minutes. Add sausage and tomatoes. Cover and simmer about 20 minutes to blend flavors. Makes about 6 servings.

MINT

Description: Mint is best described as a soothing herb. Mint plants come in so many different varieties that it is hard to choose which one to plant. There is spearmint, peppermint, chocolate, apple, and pineapple, to name a few. Leaves are dark green and range in size from one half to one inch in diameter.

Growing and Maintenance of Mint

Mint practically grows itself, in fact, if it has a mind to, it will fill your entire garden. Some gardeners recommend growing your mint in pots to prevent this hostile takeover. The mint at my cabin has wandered into the dog pen, which makes a nice contrast to what is normally left there.

Personally, I let my mint run wild for a while and then trim it back to the ground. I leave a few roots intact in the area where I want the mint to grow and before I know it, it returns again, healthier than ever. Insect enemies can include cabbage loopers and whiteflies. Cats can also be attracted to mint so if you find cat hair in your mint bed, you know who to blame. These are hardy herbs as even the gopher that has been avoiding me can't seem to kill it. Where it snows it can be expected to die back, but don't think for a minute that it is dead. As soon as warm temperatures return, so will the mint. This is an excellent first herb for any gardener.

Harvesting Mint

In mild climates, mint can be harvested year-round. Pick individual leaves or cut the entire stem. Remember, it is hardy and can sacrifice a lot of foliage and still bounce back.

Mint Preservation

Mint can be dried the same as any herb. As it is an abundant perennial and grows year-round in the Southwest, we do not dry it at our house. If you want to preserve mint, harvest before it flowers. After washing stems, tie and hang in a dark, dry, ventilated space. Mint can also be dried by removing the leaves from the stems and air drying on a clean counter or baking sheet.

When dry, crush leaves by rolling in newspapers or paper towels (See: Basil Preservation). Freezing mint into ice cubes is not very appealing. The mint flavor is there, but it results in a blackish-green product and is not recommended.

Mint Uses

⚘ Peppermint tea is an excellent remedy for indigestion. Pack a mug with leaves and cover with boiling water. Steep for five minutes or more. Sweeten if desired.

❧ Excess mint plants make great gifts. While thinning plants, make sure to pull some with the roots attached. Pot in small containers. Nurture until plants perk up and pass them onto friends and neighbors.

❧ Mint makes a refreshing iced tea. Make your tea as usual, adding a few leaves while steeping the tea. Cool, add ice, enjoy.

Mint Recipes

Hot Spiced Tea

This beverage concentrate is delicious on a cold winter evening. It will keep for several days in the refrigerator.

1 cup water

3 black tea bags

4-5 **mint leaves**

½ teaspoon allspice

¼ cup lemon juice

¾ cup orange juice

Sweetener to taste

Bring water to boil and add tea, mint, and allspice. Allow to steep for 10 minutes. Strain and add lemon and orange juice. To serve, combine ¼ cup tea concentrate with 6 ounces boiling water. Makes 8 servings.

§§§

Lightening Lemonade

This recipe came from my mom and God only knows where she found it. It is so refreshing on a hot summer day. Add the vodka and pretty soon you'll forget how hot it is.

1 cup sugar

1 cup water

½ cup fresh lemon juice

2 cups club soda

Several ice cube trays, any shape or size

mint leaves to taste, plus garnish

Vodka to taste

Mix sugar, water, and juice until sugar is dissolved. Freeze in ice cube trays. When ready to serve, combine ice cubes and mint and blend until slushy. Fill a glass half full with mint slush and top with soda and vodka. Serve with a sprig of fresh mint.

≋≋≋

Mint Chocolate Chip Ice Cream

Homemade mint ice cream has a delicate flavor and is a great way to utilize your mint. Why not try using chocolate mint in this recipe? You can adjust the amount of mint and chocolate to personal preference, but don't eliminate the egg yolks. Yolks help emulsify the mixture and thicken the ice cream. It is also an important ingredient to reduce the formation of ice crystals in the cream. However, most of the time the ice cream doesn't last long enough to form crystals.

½ cup packed **mint leaves**

⅔ cup sugar

⅛ teaspoon salt

3 cups half and half cream

2 egg yolks

⅓ cup dark chocolate, grated. We use Ghirardelli chocolate.

First, prepare the sugar. In a food processor, combine mint with sugar until finely chopped.

In a medium-size saucepan, combine milk, salt, and sugar with mint. Warm cream until sugar dissolves; it will begin to get frothy around the edges of the pan and should take about 5 minutes.

Separate yolks from eggs and whip in food processor. Add a small amount of the cream to the yolks and continue beating until well blended. Add egg mixture to cream in pan and warm to 170-175 degrees.

Strain leaves from cream, pressing with a spoon to sieve tiny pieces of mint into the cream. Cool to room temperature then chill cream for at least 4 hours before churning. If you skip this step your ice cream could get very hard and crusty when it is frozen.

When ice cream is churning, thick, and is nearly done, add chocolate. Serve immediately or continue chilling in freezer to allow cream to harden. Makes about one delicious quart.

☙☙☙

Minted Hummus

Mint adds the most surprising flavor to this healthy snack.

16 ounces canned or cooked garbanzo beans, drained

2 cloves garlic, coarsely chopped

2 tablespoons lemon juice

¼ teaspoon salt

3 tablespoons **mint leaves,** chopped**,** plus mint sprigs for garnish

¼ cup virgin olive oil

1 tablespoon red wine vinegar

¼ cup red onion, chopped fine

Combine beans, garlic, lemon juice, salt, mint, oil, and vinegar and blend in food processor until smooth. Fold in chopped onion. Garnish with mint sprigs. Serve with bread cubes, crackers, pita, or fresh vegetables. Makes about 2 cups.

OREGANO

Description: Oregano is a trailing herb with round, dime-size leaves on long, wandering, woody stems. It pairs nicely with basil in rich, tomato sauces. The Greeks are credited with being the first to use oregano as a medicinal herb, to crown their heads, provide psychic dreams, and bring happiness.

Growing and Maintenance of Oregano

Our oregano covers a small sloping hill in our herb garden. It will freely root where the stem lays down on the ground and is an excellent ground cover. In our warm climate, oregano is a perennial so we are blessed with fresh oregano all year.

However, it is also very cold hardy and has returned year after year, despite snow in our mountain cabin. Oregano is said to produce a stronger flavor when provided full sun, but don't take that chance if the summer heat is too intense for young plants. Oregano does not require a lot of water or fertilizer. Controlling its growth is probably the biggest issue, so shaping and trimming on a regular basis will keep it from wandering too far from home.

Harvesting Oregano

Oregano can be harvested fresh at any time. It is most abundant in the spring when new growth is apparent. Watch closely and as small buds begin to form on the tip of the branches, it's time to pick your oregano. All herbs reach their peak flavor right before they push out their flowers.

Oregano Preservation

Collect large, long stems containing healthy, full leaves. Rinse in cool water to remove dirt and debris. Tie branches into bundles and hang in a dry, dark place. Small leaves are easily removed from branches after drying. Take several branches at a time and roll in newspaper or paper towels to crush leaves from stems. Because these are small leaves, they can also be stripped from the branch directly after harvesting and left to dry on a large baking sheet or clean counter.

Oregano Uses

❧ Top fresh, warm Italian bread with olive oil and a sprinkling of dried oregano. Intoxicating!

❧ Oregano has powerful antibiotic qualities. For sinus inflammation and a stuffy nose, pour boiling water over clean, fresh oregano, make a tent over your head with a bath towel, inhale and relax.

❧ Don't use too much oregano in your cooking as it can make foods bitter.

❧ Oregano makes a beautiful ground cover in your garden.

Oregano Recipes

Mexican Tortilla Soup

2 tablespoons virgin olive oil

½ cup diced onion

2 cloves garlic, minced

3 boneless, skinless chicken thighs

3½ cups chicken broth

16 ounces canned tomatoes and juice

1 cup tomato sauce

4 ounces diced green chilies or ½ cup diced fresh chili peppers

1 cup frozen or canned corn (drain if using canned corn)

1 teaspoon dried **oregano**

½ teaspoon cumin

4-5 corn tortillas

Oil for frying

¼ cup **cilantro**, chopped

4-6 ounces cheddar cheese, grated

In a 2-quart pan, sauté onion and garlic until onions are translucent and slightly brown. Add broth and bring to a boil. In the meantime, remove all visible fat from chicken thighs. Add thighs to broth and simmer until chicken is no longer pink. Remove chicken to cool.

Add tomatoes, tomato sauce, green chilies, corn, oregano, and cumin to broth. Dice chicken and add to soup. Cover and simmer 20 minutes.

In the meantime, prepare fried tortillas. Cut corn tortillas into ¼ inch strips. In very hot oil, fry tortillas until they are crispy and lightly browned. Remove and drain on paper towels to absorb excess oil.

To serve: layer tortilla chips in the bottom of serving bowls and ladle soup into bowls. Sprinkle with cilantro and cheese. Makes 4 servings.

Eggplant Parmigiana

3 tablespoons virgin olive oil

½ cup onion, chopped

2 cloves sliced garlic

1 pound lean ground beef or chicken

6 ounces tomato paste

2 teaspoons dried **oregano**

1 teaspoon dried **basil**

1 teaspoon salt

¼ teaspoon black pepper

2 teaspoons sugar

1 cup water

1 large eggplant, sliced thin

2 eggs, beaten

¾ cup seasoned bread crumbs

1 cup grated Parmesan cheese, divided

Olive oil for frying

8 ounces mozzarella cheese, grated

In a large skillet, sauté onion, garlic, and ground meat until meat is no longer pink. Add tomato paste, oregano, basil, salt, pepper, sugar, and water. Simmer for 20 minutes.

Prepare a 13 x 9-inch baking pan oiling sides and bottom of dish.

Dip eggplant in egg bath and coat in bread crumbs. In a separate frying pan sauté eggplant in olive oil until brown on both sides. Add additional oil as needed. As eggplant finishes browning, layer half of eggplant in the prepared baking dish. Sprinkle with Parmesan cheese. Spoon half of the meat mixture over the eggplant, followed by half of the mozzarella. Continue the same process for the next layer.

Bake uncovered at 375 degrees for 25 minutes. If casserole or cheese topping browns too fast, cover with a loose tent of aluminum foil until cooking is complete. Makes 6-8 servings.

☙☙☙

Vegetable Lasagna

9 lasagna noodles

2 tablespoons virgin olive oil

1 cup onion, chopped fine

1 cup carrots, chopped fine

2 cups ricotta cheese

2 eggs

¼ cup Parmesan cheese

1 teaspoon dried **oregano**

1 bunch fresh spinach, chopped into bite size pieces

14-15 ounces of your favorite prepared spaghetti sauce (or use Nana's Sugo under Basil)

1 cup diced tomato

1½ cup mozzarella cheese, shredded, about 6-8 ounces

Lightly oil a 13 x 9-inch baking pan. In a large pot of boiling, salted water, boil noodles according to package directions. Noodles will handle better if slightly underdone. Drain, rinse under cool water, and set aside.

In a medium size pan, sauté onions and carrots

until onions are translucent, about five minutes. Add spinach and continue cooking another five minutes. While vegetables are finishing, combine ricotta, eggs, Parmesan cheese, and oregano in a small bowl and set aside.

Ladle a small amount of sauce in the bottom of the baking pan. Top with 3 noodles, laying them side by side to fit in the pan. Top with more sauce. Scatter half the vegetables over the noodles and sauce, spreading evenly. Do the same with half the ricotta mix and finish with half the mozzarella. Repeat with the next layer. Complete the casserole by layering the last 3 noodles on top, followed by sauce, tomatoes, and mozzarella.

Oil the underside of aluminum foil which will be used to cover the casserole. Bake at 350 degrees for 40-45 minutes. Casserole should be bubbling and hot before removing from oven. Allow to sit for 10-15 minutes so liquid is absorbed. Delicious with garlic bread and a green salad with fresh herbs! Makes 6-8 servings.

PARSLEY

Description: Parsley is a very common herb and is often sold in small bunches at the grocery store. It is very inexpensive at the grocer but nothing compares to picking your own organic parsley and bringing it in the kitchen to prepare with your meal. It has a fresh fragrance all its own, adds color to any dish, and is exceptionally high in vitamins A and C. There are many superstitions about parsley that have persisted for hundreds of years. Some cultures believe that parsley seeds are slow to sprout, " 'cause they have to visit the devil nine times." Others say you should never transplant parsley plants from one home to another because it brings bad luck. I'm thinking they are looking for an excuse as to why they couldn't grow parsley!

Growing and Maintenance of Parsley

In a warm climate, parsley will do best in partial shade. In cooler climates, parsley can tolerate full sun. The seeds look very similar to carrot seeds so it's not a surprise they are related. Italian parsley has a flat leaf and is often preferred for its impressive culinary flavor. Curly leaf is flavorful and makes an attractive presentation as a garnish. Choose an heirloom variety that works best for you.

Plant your seeds when the danger of frost has passed. Parsley likes loamy, rich soil. Keep the soil moist until the seeds sprout. Don't get discouraged as this could take some time. As the parsley grows, watering can be reduced. When the parsley plant ages, the leaves will become less potent and useful. Eventually it will flower and go to seed. Let it! If you're lucky, you may get two crops in one year.

Harvesting Parsley

Harvest your parsley as soon as the plant is big enough to sacrifice a few leaves. Collect from the outside of the plant, allowing the center to continue to fill out. Cut close to the base of the stem of the parsley. Some cooks include the stem in their cooking as they also hold a lot of flavor. If you are using the stems in stews or soups, tie them with twine before cooking so they are easily removed when you serve. You can also use a stock bag for the stems (See: Tools).

Parsley Preservation

To dry parsley, rinse in cool water to remove any dust and debris. Tie the ends of the parsley stems and shake off any excess water. Hang the plants in a dry, well-ventilated, dark area. Once the leaves become crispy, the leaves may be crushed and removed from the stems (See the description under basil). Parsley leaves can also be hand-picked and dried on a baking sheet for several days. To test for dryness, crumble a leaf between two fingers. It should easily break into small pieces. If not, or if it feels "rubbery," let it dry for a couple more days.

Parsley Uses

⚘ Large portions of parsley (such as pesto) or parsley oil can initiate uterine contractions. Do not use huge quantities while pregnant, but after delivery it can help tone the uterus.

⚘ Ancient Romans wore a garland of parsley on their heads during feasts to prevent intoxication. My thought is that it never hurts to try and would be a great conversation starter at any party.

⚘ Parsley is not useful in controlling bad breath. Instead, try green tea.

Parsley Recipes

Chuck Wagon Casserole

Most every time my children had an overnight guest, Chuck Wagon had to be on the dinner menu. It was a fast, easy macaroni dish that children and adults enjoy. It got to a point where guests were asking for it by name! The original recipe called for black olives, but if kids don't like olives, they are easily omitted.

1 pound lean ground beef

16 ounces canned corn with liquid (It's not the same made with frozen corn.)

16 ounces tomato sauce

2 cups water

1 teaspoon dried **parsley**

1 cup elbow macaroni

8 ounces cheddar cheese, grated

Optional: 4 ounces black, sliced olives

In a large skillet, brown ground beef until no longer pink. Drain fat. Add corn, tomato sauce, water, and parsley and bring to boil. Stir in macaroni, cover and simmer until macaroni is tender and all liquid has been absorbed. Turn into oiled 13 x 9-inch baking dish. Top with cheese and olives. Cover and bake at 375 degrees for 25-30 minutes or until casserole is bubbling and cheese has melted. To avoid having the cheese stick to the foil, coat foil with a small amount of oil before covering pan. Makes 6 servings depending on appetites and seconds!

⸙⸙⸙

Fettuccini with Onions and Bacon

½ cup sweet, Vidalia onions, chopped

3 slices bacon, cut into thin strips (To reduce fat use Canadian bacon.)

1 clove garlic, minced

1 tablespoon butter

½ cup whipping cream

⅓ cup grated Parmesan cheese, divided

2 tablespoons fresh **parsley**, chopped

½ teaspoon black pepper

¼ teaspoon salt

½ pound fettuccine, cooked and drained

In a large, deep saucepan, sauté onions and bacon until onions are translucent and bacon is crispy. Drain excess bacon fat. Add cream, 3 tablespoons Parmesan cheese, parsley, pepper, salt, and pasta. Toss lightly to blend ingredients. Top servings with remaining Parmesan cheese. Makes 3-4 servings.

☙❦❧

Herbed London Broil

The ideal way to prepare this steak is on the grill or under the broiler in a seasoned cast iron pan. Otherwise use a broiling pan.

½ cup butter

¼ cup fresh **parsley**, chopped

¼ cup onion, minced

2 tablespoons Worcestershire sauce

1 teaspoon black pepper

½ teaspoon dry mustard

2 tablespoons lemon juice

1, 2½ pound flank steak, 1½ inches thick

Three hours before cooking, in a small saucepan, melt butter and add parsley, onion, Worcestershire sauce, pepper, mustard, and lemon juice. Reserve 2-3 tablespoons of seasoned butter and set aside.

In a baking pan, use remaining butter to baste steak on both sides. Cover and put in refrigerator to allow seasonings to marinate steak.

When ready to cook, heat seasoned cast iron pan in hot oven. To cook steak in skillet or on grill, brush with seasoned butter, cook 6-7 minutes per side and baste frequently. Internal temperatures for desired doneness are as follows:

Mooing to rare- 120-130 degrees

Medium rare- 135 degrees

Medium- 140 degrees

Medium Well- 150 degrees

Well to Boot Leather- 160 degrees

Remove steak to cutting board and slice against the grain of the meat. Top with warmed, seasoned butter and serve immediately. Makes 6 servings.

Spinach Frittata

This is a delicious meatless dish I like to prepare when my laying hens are working into overtime and there are lots of fresh eggs. Serve with garlic bread and a mixed green salad.

3 tablespoons virgin olive oil

½ cup onions, sliced

10 eggs

1 bunch fresh spinach, chopped fine

⅓ cup grated Parmesan cheese

1 tablespoon **fresh parsley,** chopped fine

1 clove garlic, minced

1 teaspoon salt

Black pepper to taste

In a small skillet, heat olive oil and brown onions until translucent, about 5 minutes.

In a large bowl, whisk eggs. Add spinach, cheese, parsley, garlic, salt and pepper. Add prepared onions and turn into oiled, 8 x 8 baking dish. Bake at 350 degrees for 20-25 minutes or until top is set. Use a spatula to check under frittata for doneness and browning. If eggs are still too soft, continue baking a few more minutes. Allow to cool slightly before cutting into 6 portions.

ROSEMARY

Description: Rosemary grows as a bush or a trailing vine with dark green leaves and is often used as an ornamental plant in landscaping. It grows on long, woody stems with a spike-shaped leaf, about one-half inch long. In the spring, rosemary produces delicate blue flowers.

Growing and Maintenance of Rosemary

The only time I ever had a rosemary bush give up and die on me is when it was over-powered by nearby plants and did not get any sunlight. In a word, these plants are indestructible, again—an excellent plant for beginners. Additional care requires they do not sit in soggy soil or get root bound in a container. If your rosemary plant is browning, it is stressed and the above-mentioned conditions should be addressed to save the plant.

Rosemary should not be exposed to freezing temperatures. A surprise freeze may not kill it, but if you live in snow country, you will need to grow your rosemary in a container that can be relocated when winter rolls around.

Trimming your rosemary plant will result in a dense, bushy plant. If it is not necessary to keep it contained, let it run free!

Harvesting Rosemary

When harvesting your rosemary, pick full branches with leaves in prime condition. If your plant is small, you can still harvest a few fresh stems while it is growing, but wait until it is big and full before harvesting for preservation. When using fresh rosemary, leaves can be snipped from the stems with scissors and used directly in your cooking.

Rosemary Preservation

Rinse branches in cool water to remove dust and shake off excess water. Because rosemary dries quickly, this herb can be tied in larger bundles. Hang in a cool, dark place. When completely dry, roll stems in a newspaper or paper towels to remove leaves. I go a step further and grind my rosemary in a small coffee grinder to make rosemary powder. If you are using the same grinder for coffee, be sure to clean the grinder thoroughly as rosemary has such a powerful fragrance. I keep a grinder on hand that is dedicated to my herbs and seeds. Hand grinders can also be used to powder or mince herbs. (See the grinder I use under *Tools.*)

Rosemary Uses

≉ Set your holiday table with rosemary. Choose red and green napkins. Fold the napkin under and tie with natural twine or raffia. Slip a small stem of rosemary under the twine. It fills the air with an evergreen fragrance.

⚘ Fresh rosemary can settle anxiety. Take a few stems and rub it between your fingers to release the fragrance. Inhale! The scent of rosemary imparts a calming effect and quiets frayed nerves.

⚘ Stuff a whole chicken with rosemary branches before baking in the oven. Pack a few fresh stems under the wings, legs, and skin. Lay a few wet rosemary cuttings on the grill and put your pork chops on top for a delicious herbal barbeque.

Rosemary Recipes

Joseph's Rosemary Carrots

This is a regular at holiday gatherings and will please the taste buds of young and old. It is such a simple recipe but one that is always requested.

1 pound of small baby carrots. If using regular carrots, peel and cut into 2 to 3-inch wedges.

3 tablespoons butter

2-3 tablespoons fresh **rosemary,** chopped fine.

Salt to taste

Cook carrots in salted water until fork tender,

about 10 minutes. Drain and set aside. In the same saucepan, sauté **rosemary** in butter on low heat for 5-10 minutes. Butter will brown slightly but watch closely to avoid burning. Add carrots and continue heating for 5 minutes or until carrots are glossy and lightly browned. Makes 5-6 servings.

꙲꙲꙲

Grilled Rosemary Potatoes

I like to use this recipe when we are grilling outdoors, but it is even better when you are camping and don't want to spend a lot of time on clean-up.

4 medium size red potatoes, unpeeled, sliced thin

1 small onion, sliced thin

¼ cup olive oil

2 teaspoons dried or fresh **rosemary**

Heavy duty aluminum foil

Tear off 4 large pieces of aluminum foil. Divide potatoes and onions equally on each piece of foil. Drizzle with 1 tablespoon of olive oil and sprinkle with rosemary. Tightly wrap into packets by bringing two sides together and folding edges over several times to make an envelope. Fold each end in the same way. Place on grill, turning packets frequently. Allow 45 minutes for grilling. Check the potatoes for tenderness by piercing through foil with a fork. Makes 4 servings.

❦❦❦

Michigan Bean Soup

A few years ago, we were vacationing in Michigan and had the most delicious bean soup. While still sitting at the table, I wrote down all the wonderful flavors I was sensing. I came home and reproduced the recipe adding a little rosemary to my version of this hearty soup.

½ cup butter, divided

½ cup onion, chopped

½ cup celery, chopped

1 teaspoon fresh or dried **rosemary**

1¾ cups ham, chopped into ¼ inch pieces

6 tablespoons flour

2 cups unsalted chicken broth

2 cups canned navy beans

½ teaspoon Old Bay seasoning

¼ teaspoon smoke flavoring

In a large saucepan, melt 2 tablespoons butter and add onions, celery, rosemary, and ham. Sauté until vegetables are translucent and slightly caramelized. Remove from pan and set aside. In the same pan melt remaining butter. Add flour and blend into butter. Add chicken broth, beans, Old Bay seasoning, ham and vegetable mix, and smoke flavoring. Simmer for 15-20 minutes to blend flavors. Makes 5-6 servings.

SAGE

Description: Sage has a thick, greyish-green leaf that can range in size from one to two inches in width. It does well in cold weather, resists frost damage, and is often used in poultry dishes.

Growing and Maintenance of Sage

Sage can grow in part shade or full sun, depending on the summer temperature in your region. My two sage plants grow in part-shade due to the excessive heat in the desert. Water your sage regularly but do not let it sit in soggy soil. Older plants will develop woody stems that should be trimmed back annually. Sage has a tendency to get a little unruly so trimming a few branches up from the ground will help present a neater appearance. Fertilizers are not required for your sage plant. A healthy dose of compost should keep your plant happy and productive.

I have never had luck collecting seeds from my sage plants. If you have a hardy plant and want more, try propagating new plants from cuttings. To do this, cut several 2-3 inch pieces of a branch, dampen the ends, and dip in a root stimulating product. These are available at any garden shop and are a safe hormone-type product that stimulates growth. Make sure all leaves are removed from the stems except for a couple at the top. Place stems in small containers filled with potting soil. Keep moist and wait about six weeks for roots to grow. Transplant into larger containers to allow for growth and enjoy your new sage plants. (Also see Cutting Globes, under *Tools*.)

Harvesting Sage

Sage is a great herb used fresh or dried. Pick leaves as needed or collect branches when drying large quantities for storage. Harvest before plants start to flower.

Sage Preservation

Sage leaves are fuzzy so dirt and debris attaches easily. Thoroughly wash your herbs before using in cooking or drying and check the back of the leaves. Bundle and hang to dry in a cool, dark place. Allow for extra drying time with these thick leaves. When dry, crush stems between newspapers or paper towels and collect leaves. Take a handful of leaves and rub between palms to break leaves into small pieces that can be measured for recipes.

Sage Uses

⚜ Native Americans and spiritualists often use sage in a cleansing ceremony as a "smudge stick." A smoldering bundle of sage is taken room to room to clear the home of negative energy.

🌿 Clinical studies have demonstrated that sage has a positive effect on memory and concentration.

🌿 Make an infusion (similar to a tea) of sage leaves and use as a hair rinse for shiny, soft hair. Bring water to a boil, pour over sage leaves and allow to infuse for 10 minutes. Remove leaves and cool.

Sage Recipes

Chicken Noodle Casserole

This is my ultimate comfort food and a great way to use leftover chicken. To reduce the fat in this recipe, remove skin and all visible fat before cooking chicken, use a reduced-fat canned soup, use a reduced-fat sour cream and eliminate the butter with the crackers. Still delicious!

4 chicken thighs or 3 cups diced, cooked chicken

3 cups egg noodles, about 6 ounces dry

1 can condensed cream of mushroom soup

2 tablespoons dried **sage**

⅔ cup sour cream

¼ cup milk

2 tablespoons butter

1 cup crumbled crackers

Place chicken in a medium size pot, cover with water and bring to a boil. Skim foam as it forms. When chicken is no longer pink, remove to plate and allow to cool. Save broth and cut chicken into ½ inch pieces.

Bring chicken broth to boil. Add noodles to boiling broth and prepare according to package instructions. Drain, rinse in cool water and set aside. In a medium-size bowl combine mushroom soup, sage, sour cream, and milk.

Add chicken and noodles to soup mixture and combine all ingredients. Pour into an oiled or buttered 9 x 13- inch baking dish. Melt butter in a small skillet. Add crackers, turning frequently to lightly brown. Top casserole with crackers and bake at 350 degrees for 25-30 minutes. Makes approximately 6 servings.

☙ ☙ ☙

Cornbread Dressing

There are no holidays at our house that do not include this dressing. In fact, I usually have to make two batches so my son can take one home. You can make it in one day but I prefer to get all the ingredients ready and then prepare it so it comes out fresh from the oven, just in time for the turkey and other fixings. I always try to cook from scratch, but a boxed cornbread saves time and does not alter the recipe.

The day before making the dressing, prepare the cornbread:

¾ cup cornmeal

1½ cups flour

1½ tablespoons sugar

1 tablespoon baking powder

1 teaspoon salt

⅓ cup oil or shortening

1 egg

1¼ cups milk

Combine dry ingredients. If using shortening, cut into dry ingredients. If using oil, combine with egg and milk. Mix egg and milk with dry ingredients until blended. Spread into an 8 by 8-inch buttered baking dish. Bake at 400 degrees for 30-35 minutes. Cool and remove from pan. Crumble into small pieces.

The vegetables may also be prepared the day before:

4 tablespoons butter

2 cups celery, diced ½ inch, about 3-4 stalks

2 cups onion, diced ½ inch, about 1 medium onion

2 cups apples, diced ½ inch, about 2 apples

In large skillet, melt butter and add vegetables. Sauté on medium heat until tender, about 20 minutes.

To finish:

6 eggs

3-4 cups chicken stock

6 cups diced Italian or French bread, about 7 slices

3 tablespoons dried **sage**

2 teaspoons salt

½ teaspoon black pepper

Prepared cornbread

Prepared vegetables

In a large bowl whisk eggs into stock. Add bread, sage, salt, pepper, and prepared cornbread and vegetables. Gently combine ingredients. Loosely pack into a buttered 13 x 9-inch baking pan. Cover and bake at 350 degrees for 50-55 minutes. Uncover during the last 10 minutes to brown. Makes 12-15 servings.

≋≋≋

Pasta with Squash and Sage

This is a healthy vegetarian dish and makes a hearty meal on a cool, fall night.

1 medium butternut squash

⅓ cup olive oil, divided

¾ pound pasta or 12 ounces, cooked

3 tablespoons pine nuts

2 cloves garlic, sliced

2 tablespoons **fresh sage,** chopped fine

Salt and pepper to taste

Grated Parmesan cheese

Prepare squash by peeling, cut in half, seed, and dice into ½ inch pieces. Toss with 2 tablespoons of olive oil to coat squash and spread on baking sheet in single layer. If desired, sprinkle with salt. Broil on low for 20-25 minutes until squash is lightly browned.

In a large, deep skillet, bring water to boil and cook pasta according to package directions. Drain, rinse to cool and set aside.

In the same skillet, combine remaining oil with pine nuts and garlic. Sauté until nuts and garlic are lightly browned. Stir in sage, continue cooking for 1 minute and set aside.

Combine squash and pasta with nuts, garlic, and seasoned oil. Toss to combine ingredients. Top with grated cheese. Makes 5-6 servings.

THYME

Description: My favorite thyme (pronounced "time") is lemon thyme. Pungent, almost invigorating, thyme is a refreshing herb that is available in many different varieties. English and lemon thyme are most common. The emerald green plant has very tiny leaves on long, wispy stems. Of all the herbs, this one is quite delicate.

Growing and Maintenance of Thyme

Thyme tolerates drought and does not like wet soil. In climates with very cold weather it is recommended to heavily mulch the thyme plants. It welcomes trimming and can even be shaped. *Bonnie*

Plants offers these great tips for trimming thyme: "Pinching the tips of the stems keeps plants bushy, but stop clipping about a month before the first frost of fall to make sure that new growth is not too tender going into the cool weather. Cut thyme back by one third in spring, always cutting above points where you can see new growth, never below into the leafless woody stem."

Harvesting Thyme

Thyme can be harvested at any time, but it is most flavorful just before tiny white flowers emerge. Watch carefully and you can see small buds forming on the tips of the stems. For small amounts, harvest as needed. To preserve large quantities of thyme, it may be best to wait until spring when trimming the plant.

Thyme Preservation

To preserve large quantities of thyme, clip long stems with vigorous, healthy leaf growth. Rinse in cool water and shake off excess water. At this point the herb may be tied into bundles for drying or laid out on a baking sheet to air dry indoors. Because the leaves are so small, it will dry in a very short period of time. To collect dried leaves, turn the stem upside down, pinch the stem at the top, and pull down on the branch. You can also roll it in newspaper or a paper towel as suggested with other herbs. Remove small sticks and store the remaining herb in an air-tight container. Thyme will retain all its fresh flavor, even in a dried state.

Thyme Uses

≋ Add fresh thyme to butter or mayonnaise for a special dressing.

≋ Ancient Greeks burned thyme inside the home to discourage stinging insects.

≋ Thyme, as with most herbs, can be added to vinegars while still on the stem to enhance the flavor. Allow at least two weeks for the flavor to infuse the vinegar.

Thyme Recipes

Salmon Melt

A light, healthy, open-face sandwich, rich in Omega 3s. I prefer using fresh thyme in this recipe.

1 6-ounce can pink salmon

¼ cup mayonnaise

1 tablespoon fresh **thyme**

3 slices sour dough bread, lightly toasted

2 slicing tomatoes, cut thin

3 slices sharp cheddar cheese

In a small bowl, combine salmon, mayonnaise and thyme. Spread evenly on sliced bread. Top with thin slices of tomato and one slice of cheese. Broil on low for several minutes until cheese melts over bread. Makes 3 servings.

※※※

Stuffed Chicken Breasts

4 boneless, skinless chicken breasts

Salt and pepper to taste

1 cup seasoned croutons

¼ teaspoon orange zest

4 ounces mandarin oranges, drained

½ teaspoon dried **thyme**

2 tablespoons onion, grated

2 tablespoons minced pecans

2 tablespoons butter, melted

1 cup orange juice, divided

On waxed paper, pound and flatten chicken breast. Season with salt and pepper to taste. In a small bowl combine croutons, orange zest, oranges, thyme, onion, pecans. Drizzle with butter and 3 tablespoons, mix to blend ingredients.

Put ¼ of mixture on each chicken fillet, fold over and secure with a toothpick. Place in baking pan and spoon remaining orange juice over chicken. Cover and bake at 375 degrees for 30 minutes. Uncover and bake another 20-30 minutes or until stuffed chicken reaches an internal temperature of

185 degrees and no pink color remains. Remaining juice in pan may be thickened with cornstarch to make a sauce. Makes 4 servings.

⁂

Beef in a Bag

In a hurry and no time to make dinner? This is a fast way to prepare an entire meal in the oven. If you are expecting a busy day, prepare this the day before and have it ready to go when it's time to make dinner. A 7-bone roast requires a long cooking time, but once it is bagged, the oven does all the work. For added flavor, the roast and mushrooms can be browned in a hot skillet before bagging.

1, 2-3 pound 7-bone roast (7-bone because the bone is shaped in a number 7)

2 cloves garlic, sliced

Ground black pepper

2 small onions, quartered

½ pound whole baby carrots

½ pound whole mushrooms

2 potatoes, peeled and quartered

2 cloves garlic, sliced

1 teaspoon dried **thyme**

1 cup tomato juice

In a 13 x 9-inch baking dish, open oven-proof cooking bag for filling. Make slits in top of roast and stuff with garlic slices. Heavily pepper roast. Place roast in bag. Arrange onions, carrots, mushrooms, and potatoes around sides of roast. Mix thyme and tomato juice and ladle over roast. Tie bag and cut slits on top to allow steam to escape. Do not forget this step!

Bake at 300-325 degrees for 3-4 hours or until roast reaches a minimal internal temperature of 140 degrees and the vegetables are tender. The meat should separate easily with a fork. If desired, broth may be collected from the roast and thickened with a roux to make a gravy.

Roux for gravy: 2 tablespoons melted butter with 2 tablespoons flour.

HERB MIXES

These mixes can be made with your home-grown herbs. Combine all ingredients and store in an airtight container. Try to use your dried herbs and mixes within one year.

Vegetable Supreme Seasoning Mix

McCormick spices used to have an herb mix that was delicious on vegetables but a few years back they stopped making it. This is my personal creation to replace that product. In all fairness to my taste buds, I would call this a success.

There are many butter-flavored powders at the grocer. Also try *Firehouse Pantry Store* online.

This recipe makes about ½ cup:

1¼ teaspoons sesame seeds

5 teaspoons onion powder (or 1 tablespoon + 2 teaspoons)

2½ teaspoons **thyme**, dried and crushed fine

2½ teaspoons **basil**, dried and crushed fine

1¼ teaspoons turmeric

2½ tablespoons powdered butter flavoring

Combine all ingredients and store in an airtight jar. I like to save empty spice bottles and reuse them with my homegrown herbs. I use a shaker jar for this mix.

☙☙☙

Chinese Herb Mix

Techniques vary on how this mix is made, but the ingredients are consistent. Known as Chinese Five Spice Powder, this contains five distinct spices and herbs that can enhance any Asian dish or recipe using soy or teriyaki sauce. If using whole herbs to make the mix, you may want to use a sieve to remove large pieces the blender or food processor may have missed. Again, I like to use a coffee bean grinder to do the job.

1½ teaspoons peppercorns

1½ teaspoons star anise

1½ teaspoons whole cloves

1 teaspoon ground cinnamon

1½ teaspoons **fennel seed**

Grind whole herbs and spices individually to equal 1 teaspoon each. For added flavor the fennel can be toasted in a hot skillet before grinding. Use a strainer to remove all large pieces. Combine powders.

For variations on this seasoning, coriander and/or ginger can be added to the mix.

≋≋≋

Taco Mix

Customize this recipe. For a low sodium product eliminate or reduce the salt and increase your favorite herb or seasoning. Like it spicy? Increase the crushed red pepper and chili powder.

1 tablespoon onion powder

½ teaspoon garlic powder

1 teaspoon salt

½ teaspoon corn starch

¼ teaspoon crushed red pepper

1 teaspoon chili powder

1 teaspoon dried **oregano**

½ teaspoon cumin

≋≋≋

Italian Seasoning Mix

1 tablespoon dried **basil**

1 tablespoon dried **oregano**

1 tablespoon dried **parsley**

1 teaspoon dried **rosemary**

1 teaspoon dried **thyme**

½ teaspoon black pepper

≋≋≋

Poultry Seasoning

2 teaspoons dried **sage**

2 teaspoons dried **thyme**

1 teaspoon onion powder

1 teaspoon garlic powder

1 teaspoon marjoram

½ teaspoon dried **parsley**

¼ teaspoon black pepper

🌱🌱🌱

Seasoned Bread Crumbs

Around our house nothing goes to waste. Once a year I collect all the old breads I have put aside in my freezer, dice them up into small pieces and dry the bread on a baking sheet for several days. Then it goes into the grinder with my dried herbs and I usually have enough bread crumbs to last the entire year. A food processor or blender will also do the job, but the grinder will produce a more consistent crumb.

If I have dried celery leaves on hand, I will

usually push that through the grinder with the other seasonings. Dried celery leaves have a wonderful flavor and enhance the seasoned bread crumbs. To make dried celery leaves, save any leaves you would normally discard and dry on a baking sheet. This could take anywhere from 4-7 days, depending on the humidity. Store in an airtight container and use as a seasoning.

For 2 cups of bread crumbs mix with:

1 tablespoon dried **parsley**

½ teaspoon black pepper

½ teaspoon dried **basil**

½ teaspoon dried **oregano**

½ teaspoon dried **rosemary**

1 teaspoon **fennel seed**

½ teaspoon garlic powder

1 teaspoon dehydrated onions or ½ teaspoon onion powder

Optional: 1 teaspoon salt

1 teaspoon dried celery leaves

A FINAL WORD

I was five years old when I was introduced to my first vegetable garden. My father took me behind his storage shed where a solitary, 6-inch plant was growing. He had just finished planting it and told me it was an eggplant. I still remember thinking, *I don't see any eggs on that plant.* I've learned a whole lot since then.

It still amazes me to know that under specific conditions, the DNA in one tiny seed can produce an identical plant that in turn, will produce food for all of us. The same plant leaves behind yet more seeds and the cycle of life continues. It is my hope that this book inspires you to personally experience the miracles that happen when seeds, water, dirt, and sunlight come together. Nothing gives me more joy than hearing someone was moved to plant their own herbs and vegetables because of our encounter through reading one of my books or visiting my gardens.

Last week I took my three-year-old grandson out to the garden to show him the vegetables I was growing. He admired the showy purple flower on the artichoke plant, noting that they were "prickly." Bending over for a better look, he spied my red tomatoes, repeating the name slowly as he committed it to memory. He discovered a baby watermelon growing under the zucchini leaf and said, "Oh, that one will get big, big like my Daddy."

I can't wait to share that ripe, red watermelon with him and hope to inspire another future gardener. Since it is an heirloom watermelon, perhaps we will save some seeds for next summer and he can grow his own melons in his yard. When we touch the lives of others, we leave behind a small piece of ourselves and never know how it will affect that person. May my writing help you create the gardens of your dreams and be a means to explore the beauty and bounty of our planet.

About the Author:

Josephine DeFalco was born and raised in the Southwest near central Arizona. She grew up playing with horny toads, cactus wrens, and Red Racer snakes, occasionally winning a battle of grapefruit wars with the neighborhood boys.

As eating was a primary concern in her Italian family, she earned her first BS degree from the University of Missouri-Columbia in nutrition and dietetics, returning to Arizona to work as a registered dietitian. While raising her three children, she freelanced as a health editor for a local women's magazine. She earned a second BS, this time in nursing, from Arizona State University. She is also a certified EMT.

Josephine continues to write from her Arizona home, living on a small, organic, urban farm with her husband, five vegetable gardens, two dogs, and many spoiled laying hens. Her Facebook page, Best Little Organic Farm, encourages everyone to relish the wonders of growing and preserving their own nutritious foods, taking responsibility for their health and well-being, and honoring our beautiful planet

Visit Josephinedefalco.com.

Also Available from Josephine DeFalco:

Making homemade bread is easy, healthy, and comforting! *The Best Little Bread Book* takes the mystery out of creating the perfect loaf of homemade bread. With recipes developed in a home kitchen by nutritionist and author Josephine DeFalco, you'll discover how easy it is to make delicious bread, free of unhealthy, processed ingredients. Bread has been a staple of life for centuries. Baked in your own kitchen, these recipes will bring comfort and good nutrition into your home.

Available on Amazon and wherever books are sold.

Also Available from Josephine DeFalco:

Following the sudden death of her husband, Brenna McEvoy finds herself a widowed mother, and despite her privileged upbringing, must somehow find a way to survive. Brenna's only asset is her charming Victorian home which she transforms into a boarding house for local miners. The struggle of day-to-day living forces her to open her eyes to the suffering and bigotry surrounding the working class. When she falls in love with a working man, Manuel Rodriguez, and she finds herself shunned by her family and friends, she must decide to follow the rules of society or follow her heart. The nightbird's song reminds Brenna that we are strengthened by the struggles we survive—but will her resolve be enough to save her children?

Available on Amazon and wherever books are sold..

17575624R00079

Printed in Great Britain
by Amazon